Leading with Purpose

30 Empowering Tips to Transform Your Organization

By Nathan R Mitchell

Leading with Purpose
30 Empowering Tips to Transform Your Organization
Copyright 2013 by Nathan R Mitchell

ISBN 978-1491252574

Independent Publishing Platform
www.CreateSpace.com

Printed in the United States of America. All rights reserved under International Copyright Law. Cover and/or contents may not be reproduced in any form without the express written consent of the author.

Disclaimer: The advice and strategies contained in this book may not be suitable for your organization. The publisher and author shall not be liable for any loss of profit or other damages that may be incurred by implementing principles and strategies shared herein. You and your organization should consult with a professional where appropriate.

Table of Contents

What Others Are Saying...

Introduction

Leading with Purpose: *30 Empowering Tips to Transform Your Organization*

1. Lead with Purpose
2. Understand the Importance of Why!
3. Focus on your Job Description
4. Observe Behaviors, Not Attitudes
5. Assume the Role of Servant-Leader
6. Get the Right People on the Bus
7. The Missing Ingredient in Motivation
8. Capitalize on Strengths, Not Weaknesses
9. Understand the Real Cost of Turnover
10. Don't make it Difficult!
11. It's Not Always about the Money
12. Plant Seeds for the Future
13. Focus on Professional Development
14. Leadership is a TEAM Effort
15. Connection is KEY!
16. Celebrate Your Victories!

17. Be Fair to Your People
18. Leaders of Influence Win
19. Hire Partners, Not Employees
20. Foster a Culture of Innovation
21. Knowing What to Measure
22. Be Decisive and Take Action
23. Foster a Healthy Attitude
24. No "Animal Trainers" Allowed
25. Develop a Heart for Serving
26. Is Your Door Always Open?
27. The Power of "Thank You!"
28. Take Responsibility for Your Outcomes
29. Develop Core Competencies
30. Become a Mentor or Coach

About the Author

What Others Are Saying...

"Nathan Mitchell's presentations are invaluable. Nathan's genuine demeanor and sincerity connects very well with any audience, and makes his messages powerful. When attending 'Leading With Purpose' at the NALS Professional Development and Education Conference, it was apparent Nathan really cared about giving his audience useful knowledge and insight to become better leaders. As a leader, I gained a new understanding of myself and others. And, in the midst of many changes at NALS, my confidence and abilities to work on successful outcomes for the future was enhanced by his session. Thank you Nathan!" – *Karen McElroy, President-elect NALS, the Association for Legal Professionals*

"Nathan Mitchell is committed to making a difference in the world of business and the lives of others!"
– *James Malinchak, Featured on ABC's Hit TV Show Secret Millionaire, Author of 'Millionaire Entrepreneur Secrets,' and Founder of BigMoneySpeaker.com*

"Nathan's detailed research and information make it very clear the effects of purposeful-leadership on engagement in the workplace. His training was empowering and insightful. It really opened my eyes."
– Shelia Stephens, Training Specialist, Arvest Bank

"Nathan is an experienced professional dedicated to helping others. His passionate approach to this subject is absolutely inspiring!" *– Dr. Paul Chabot, Founder of Chabot Strategies LLC*

"Nathan knows what it means to overcome adversity and achieve success. He can help you do the same."
– Craig Groeschel, Founder and Senior Pastor of Lifechurch.tv

"Nathan is a breath of fresh air. His seminars provide real-world examples and practical solutions. His experience and passion about his subject matter really shines through." *– Lacey Cline, Organizational Development & Talent Management Professional*

"His insight, passion, and sincerity of purpose is rare in today's business world. If you or your team is looking to go to the next level, you need to call this guy!"
– Clay Clark, U.S. SBA Entrepreneur of the Year

"While at Missouri State University, Nathan studied management and the applications of that knowledge to business situations and problem solving. Solid leadership skills are attributes he has developed through his corporate experience and personal insight." – *Dr. Robert L. Trewatha, Professor Emeritus, Missouri State University*

"I recently attended a workshop with Nathan Mitchell. It was awesome! I came thinking I was going to spend a casual afternoon learning how to sell and grow my business; instead, Nathan showed me the true root for success in my business: Purpose! I've continued to reflect on many of Nathan's ideas since the workshop. Not only is this completely transforming my business; it's taking my team in a whole new direction! I look forward to attending more of Nathan's events!" – *Ashley Walls, Business Owner*

"Nathan Mitchell's purpose in life is to empower other people. If you want to empower your team or your organization at an upcoming event, the next call you need to place is to America's Leading Empowerment Coach™, Nathan R Mitchell!" – *Jim Whitt, Founder of Purpose Unlimited*

Introduction

I have a program that I present regularly called "Leading with Purpose." In that presentation, I talk about how many of us use terms like "Management" and "Leadership" interchangeably; however, they are entirely two different things.

I'm sure its no shock to you the world is becoming more and more complex. And the complexity of the world isn't diminishing anytime soon. Traditional methods of managing and leading others simply aren't working. New leadership styles must be developed to address the growing needs around us. Leaders today must become better, more purposeful leaders!

Unfortunately, many in the workplace today share a stereotypical view of what great leadership is. Confined by this, many have difficulty seeing themselves as leaders. As a result, the benefits they could bring to an organization are often missing or overlooked.

The old view of a single leader making all the decisions is quickly fading. In organizations today, when things are working well, it's because the team is functioning as a coherent whole toward the fulfillment of one organizational purpose. When organizations are in crisis-mode, it's often due to a lack of purpose.

When you consider purposeful leadership, it all starts with an organizational commitment to purpose. Once the purpose of the organization has been discovered, organizations can use that as a foundation for serving the client, and bringing out the best in its employees. Whether it's an elementary school, manufacturing facility, retail store, or law office, recognizing and appreciating the strengths of others, and finding ways to capitalize on them in order to fulfill the organization's purpose is crucial. Unfortunately, many organizations focus on weaknesses, and motivate employees through reward and punishment. And it simply doesn't work!

Purposeful leadership cannot be confined to special occasions or events. And we can't engage and motivate others the same way we do animals (reward and punishment). As I mentioned earlier, the world is more complex than it has ever been. These challenges present endless opportunities to enhance the organizational environment by nurturing the skillsets of both yourself and those around you.

A fundamental principle in purposeful leadership is the idea of partnering. Find ways to place experienced workers with less experienced workers; the one that understands the concepts with the one who doesn't. Partnering and mentoring helps develop the talent, skills, and leadership abilities of both. The less experienced have the opportunity to learn from the more experienced, and the knowledge that is taught is more thoroughly understood by those doing the teaching. Rather than developing peers within the organization, partnering and mentoring helps create allies, advocates, and associates within the purpose-driven organization.

The complexity of the world is not going to diminish. Traditional methods of leading and managing others are no longer working. New leadership styles must be nurtured and developed; in particular, we need organizations today that are focused on fulfilling their unique purpose, while helping employees capitalize on their strengths, not their weaknesses.

In conclusion, I will leave you with a fantastic quote from my good friend and fellow consultant, Jim Whitt –

"Without a purpose, our only motivation is reward and punishment."

Leading with Purpose

30 Empowering Tips to Transform Your Organization

Tip #1: Lead with Purpose

When I was in graduate school earning my Master's Degree in Business Administration, I very vividly remember that the #1 priority of any organization should be to maximize wealth for the shareholders. I'm not going to tell you that this isn't important; however, I will say that profit, and therefore shareholder wealth, is a byproduct of an organization that is committed to and fulfills its purpose.

Purpose accomplishes many things. First of all, organizational purpose clearly communicates why you are in business to your customers. Not only that, but having a clearly-defined purpose helps you hire people into your organization whose skill-sets are in alignment with the needs and wants of your organization.

Unfortunately, passion isn't enough. I know we hear about it a lot in books and at conferences, but passion quickly fades. An organization that is committed to purpose, on the other hand, can endure adversity, hire the right people, and succeed for the long term.

Is your organization leading with purpose, or are you focused exclusively on profits and driving shareholder wealth?

Today's Leadership Intention

"More men fail through lack of purpose than through lack of talent." – **Billy Holiday**

What 2-3 action items are you going to do today to be a more purposeful-leader?

1.

2.

3.

Tip #2: Understand the Importance of *Why!*

As people, we often do a really good job of answering questions like *How* and *What*; however, we don't ask ourselves *Why* nearly enough. And answering the question *Why* is fundamental to everything else. *Why* is the foundation for purpose, and purpose is the launching pad for success in life, business and leadership!

If I were to ask you, "Why do you do what you do?" Would you be able to answer me without hesitation? Or would you struggle a bit? You see, without a clearly defined *Why*, we often find ourselves simply "going through the motions" on the "hamster-wheel of life," without any clarity and direction.

And it's the same in business and leadership too! How could your career, your workplace, your organization, or your ability to lead be different if you focused more time answering the *Why* in lieu of the *How* and the *What?* I assure you. It would be transformational.

Do you understand the importance of *Why?*

Today's Leadership Intention

"Without a purpose, our only motivation is reward and punishment." – **Jim Whitt**

What 2-3 action items are you going to do today to be a more purposeful-leader?

1.

2.

3.

Tips #3: Focus on Your Job Description

My guess is this probably isn't in your Job Description, but it should be - especially if you are a leader. Part of your responsibility as a leader is to instill and build confidence within the members of your team. And it all starts with you. Self-confidence is the foundation from which sound leadership grows. So, with that in mind, do you have it?

I have a talk that I've given numerous times called "Self-Leadership: Getting What You Want by Doing What Others Won't." It's really a talk founded on basic success principles and professional development, but it's very applicable in the realm of leadership. Simply put, it's hard to effectively lead others if you can't effectively lead yourself. It's hard to build confidence in others, if you don't commonly do things to help build your own self-confidence.

Without confidence there is no leadership! What are you doing today to help your team members build confidence in themselves? What are you doing today to enhance your own self-confidence? They are great questions to ask!

Today's Leadership Intention

"The first responsibility of a leader is to define reality. The last is to say thank you. In between the leader is a servant." — **Max Dupree**

What 2-3 action items are you going to do today to be a more purposeful-leader?

1.

2.

3.

Tip #4: Observe Behaviors, Not Attitudes

I was in the corporate sector for over a decade with a Fortune 50 company, so I know all to well how corporations, in many cases, focus on improving attitude in the workplace. That's one of the major reasons for annual conferences. Corporations will bring everyone together for an entire week that is jam-packed with meetings, in an effort to inform, inspire, and engage the team for another year.

The problem is the impact from these meetings is short-lived. The passion, excitement, and improvement in employee morale and attitude quickly diminish. That's why organizations and leaders should be focusing on behaviors, not on attitudes.

In reality, a member of your team can have a great attitude; yet still have a negative influence on others in your organization. You see, it's impossible to witness "attitudes." Attitudes are internal. Behaviors are observable.

Focus on improving behavior, not attitude, and you will experience success.

Today's Leadership Intention

"A business is a reflection of the leader. A fish doesn't stink just from the tail, and a company doesn't succeed or fail from the bottom."
– Gary Feldmar

What 2-3 action items are you going to do today to be a more purposeful-leader?

1.

2.

3.

Tip #5: Assume the Role of Servant-Leader

Although servant-leadership has been around since the beginning of time, it has grown in popularity in recent years. Simply put, servant leaders serve those they lead. They don't manipulate them.

Organizations founded on purpose understand servant-leadership almost intrinsically. Team members become a means to fulfilling the purpose of the organization, not a means of driving bottom-line results through reward and punishment type management practices.

Reward and punishment, command and control – they simply don't work. As a leader, if you don't have any followers, well you aren't really leading, are you? Team members, however, will follow someone with the heart of a servant; someone who is devoted to serving the needs of the organization; someone who focuses on meeting the needs of those they are responsible for leading.

Today's Leadership Intention

"The ultimate responsibility of a leader is to facilitate other people's development as well as his own." – **Fred Pryor**

What 2-3 action items are you going to do today to be a more purposeful-leader?

1.

2.

3.

Tip #6: Get the Right People on the Bus

It's hard to argue the fact that organizations succeed because of people, and people alone! Jim Collins says "...Great vision without great people is irrelevant." And it's not enough having the right people on the bus; you also have to have them placed in the right positions. In fact, this is one of the things that separate great companies from average ones.

With that being said, I'm going to take it one step further and say that even a business driven by purpose without employees committed to that purpose is futile! Having the right people means having employees who are "buying-in" to the purpose of your organization. In many instances they will share the same values as you.

The right people understand the difference between working for wages, having a job or a career, and the opportunity to help an organization fulfill its purpose! A great question to ask yourself is this: Knowing what you know now about your employees, which ones would you rehire all over again? If you can't say yes to the rehire question, then more than likely they are not a good fit for your company.

It's true. The right people are critical to the success of a company, but without an organizational purpose, it's really hard to be effective in the employee selection and hiring process.

Today's Leadership Intention

"As a manager, the important thing is not what happens when you are there but what happens when you are not there." – **Kenneth Blanchard & Robert Lorber**

What 2-3 action items are you going to do today to be a more purposeful-leader?

1.

2.

3.

Tip #7: The Missing Ingredient in Motivation

In the midst of a recession, employee engagement is critical. Do your staff members know what is expected of them? Do you communicate this to them effectively? Do you have systems in place to align new applicants with the right jobs?

Studies show that only 1 in 7 employees are willing to go the "extra mile" for their company. Is this the case in your organization? And if so, what are the current and future implications of that for your business?

With 55% of employees disengaged in the workplace, disengaged workers cost the US economy $350 billion a year. The problem for many employees today is that they simply lack purpose in their life and work, and therefore they lack motivation to perform their job well.

For companies to reach full efficiency and profitability, owners and managers must help their staff members discover their purpose and further develop their unique talents and motivations to achieve overall job satisfaction and engagement.

Today's Leadership Intention

"I would rather perform at 90 percent of an excellence standard than 110 percent of an adequacy standard." **– Don Beveridge**

What 2-3 action items are you going to do today to be a more purposeful-leader?

1.

2.

3.

Tip #8: Capitalize on Strengths, Not Weaknesses

Phrases like "You can be anything you want to be," or "You can accomplish anything you set your mind to," get thrown around a lot. I heard them a lot myself growing up from friends, family, and teachers. Now, don't get me wrong, their intentions were good. I'm all for empowering people and encouraging them to pursue their strengths, but we all have our limitations. Just because a young man practices basketball fundamentals day in and day out for hours and hours, doesn't mean he will become the next Michael Jordan or Kevin Durant. There has to be a natural set of talents and strengths in place to help someone reach that kind of potential. And it's no different in the workplace. Employees and managers must focus on the unique strengths and the specific value-adding contributions each can bring to the team.

The problem is too many times we focus entirely too much on improving upon weaknesses. I was in the corporate sector for nearly a dozen years in management, and every time we gave performance reviews, weaknesses dominated the conversation. Did you know that, as a manager, when you focus on your employees' strengths, the chance for them to be actively disengaged in the workplace is only about one percent? Consider the potential that one shift in the way you lead your people could improve and impact the bottom-line.

Today's Leadership Intention

"You never know when a moment and a few sincere words can have an impact on a life."
-Zig Ziglar

What 2-3 action items are you going to do today to be a more purposeful-leader?

1.

2.

3.

Tip #9: Understand the Real Cost of Turnover

When it comes to costs, many organizations "cross their T's" and "dot their I's" – that is, unless you are talking about the costs of employee turnover.

What are the real costs of employee turnover? What does it really cost businesses to replace key personnel when they jump ship to change careers? Well, it depends on whom you ask. The calculations vary greatly from study to study and organization-to-organization, yet all are equally frightening!

The Society for Human Resource Management estimates that one $8.00 per hour employee costs an organization $3,500 in additional expenses when things like recruitment, lost productivity, and training and development are all taken into consideration.

Unfortunately, many businesses today don't take the time to implement a solution. Instead, many companies spend the bulk of their energy and resources finding ways to decrease payroll and increase sales. It's practically an oxymoron. The ironic thing is studies have shown a 10% reduction in employee turnover is worth more than a 10% increase in productivity, or a 10% increase in sales.

The question you should be asking is this: which will you choose to focus on in the coming months and years ahead?

Today's Leadership Intention

"The deepest craving of human nature is the need to feel appreciated." – **William James**

What 2-3 action items are you going to do today to be a more purposeful-leader?

1.

2.

3.

Tip #10: Don't make it Difficult!

Unfortunately, the majority of us have really been conditioned and trained to be followers, not leaders; to not challenge the Status Quo; to be ordinary, not extraordinary; to get out into the workplace, get a good job, and retire.

And perhaps this is the reason why many organizations are struggling. Perhaps our well-trained followers have made organizations stagnate; complacent; reluctant to change. It's better to have "Yes Men" and "Yes Women" than give people the opportunity to share grand ideas that could literally transform an entire organization.

The business world is more dynamic than ever before. It's constantly changing! Like it or not, organizations must learn to adapt or die. It's that simple. And given this challenging environment we both live and do business in today, it is necessary that all individuals in an organization become leaders – not just the bosses.

The most exciting part is this – the marketplace rewards it. But, from what I've seen, it's start-up firms that are really leading the marketplace and being innovative. In other words, challenging the Status Quo.

Seth Godin says "...Leadership isn't difficult, but *we've* been trained for years to avoid it…" And as a result, many organizations and industries today are trying to reinvent themselves. Don't make it difficult!

Leading with Purpose

Today's Leadership Intention

"I never criticize a player until they are first convinced of my unconditional confidence in their abilities." **– John Robinson**

What 2-3 action items are you going to do today to be a more purposeful-leader?

1.

2.

3.

Tip #11: It's Not Always about the Money

It's no shock to anyone in the business world that happy people in an organization are an essential ingredient to being successful. But what really motivates people? Traditional thinking tells us the more we pay employees, the more loyal and satisfied they are overall. In all actuality, this isn't the case.

A recent study on employee motivation revealed nearly 40% of the workforce is disengaged in their work; 90% of leaders say engagement is essential to their business; and yet 75% of organizations don't have an employee engagement strategy in place!

Engaging members of your team can be difficult. Individual values differ greatly person-to-person. And it's values that are the driving force behind our behaviors; in other words, what motivates us to perform in the workplace.

When you look at an employee's education, skills and training, it tells us WHAT they can do. Their behaviors tell us HOW they do it. Their values tell us WHY they do what they do – an essential ingredient to knowing what motivates them intrinsically.

Understanding the *why* in your organization is important, but it's equally important for your team members as well. Help them find they *why*, and they will feel empowered!

Today's Leadership Intention

"A total commitment is paramount to reaching the ultimate in performance." – **Tom Flores**

What 2-3 action items are you going to do today to be a more purposeful-leader?

1.

2.

3.

Tip #12: Plant Seeds for the Future

You hear a lot of talk about organizational vision and mission statements in the business world, but not a lot about purpose. And purpose helps plant seeds for future growth.

An organization's purpose provides a vivid picture of the future and serves as a guide for the decisions made in the day-to-day operations of the business. There are three elements I'd like to share that help make up a purposeful organization:

A Significant Purpose: A clear purpose for your company's existence will add clarity to your organization.

A Clear Picture Of The Future: As leaders it's easy to focus on the end result and neglect the process of getting there. A purpose-driven organization can stay focused despite adversity and hardships.

Clearly stated Core-values: Your company's core-values have a significant impact on the perceived image of your organization. Your organization's values serve as guidelines on how your company should pursue its purpose.

Purpose is of vital importance to the long-term success of any organization. Is purpose alive and well in your business? Do you talk about it? Do you live it? Are you passionate about it? Are your employees?

Leading with Purpose

Today's Leadership Intention

"Believe that you will succeed. Believe it firmly, and you will then do what it necessary to bring success about." **– Dale Carnegie**

What 2-3 action items are you going to do today to be a more purposeful-leader?

1.

2.

3.

Tip #13: Focus on Professional Development

Unless you've been living inside a bubble, it shouldn't shock you that many organizations are running leaner today than they have in years past. The problem is the more lean organizations run, the more layoffs tend to take place, and the more salary cuts seem to occur. Unfortunately, it's a double-edged sword, because these challenges often affect engagement negatively in the workplace.

In light of these challenges, it's necessary for organizations to have an increased focus on professional and self-development. One of the ways to accomplish this is through hosting a professional development workshop for members of your staff. The end result: increased communication, and more effective, efficient, and engaged employees.

For example, hosting a workshop on Behavioral Analysis, which we offer, will accomplish the following in your organization:

- Employees Will Have an Increased Understanding of Self
- Employees Will Have an Increased Understanding of Others
- Your Organization Will Experience Increased Communication
- Your Organization Will Experience Increased Productivity

Today's Leadership Intention

"If you want to change attitudes, start with a change in behavior." **– William Glasser**

What 2-3 action items are you going to do today to be a more purposeful-leader?

1.

2.

3.

Tip #14: Leadership is a TEAM Effort

What is great leadership? It's a very valid question, and a tough one to answer sometimes in a tough business and economic climate.

For one reason or another today it seems CEOs and corporate executives tend to get a lot of the credit when a company succeeds or has great results under their tenure. All you have to do is go to your local bookstore, look in the business publications section, and you will count many executives fronting the pages of today's top business magazines.

When you think about it, we've really turned high-level executives (especially those of major corporations) into icons and rock stars. The problem with this is we often ignore the front line employees and mid-level managers responsible for executing the overall vision and strategy in the field. And in my opinion, this is the team of people really responsible for ensuring the long-term success of an organization.

Don't get me wrong; you have to have top leadership. It's the nature of business, and it's also the natural way of things. With that being said, it worries me when we attribute success to the work of any one person. Leadership is really a team effort - the combined efforts of many, honorable people, working toward the fulfillment of one organizational purpose!

Today's Leadership Intention

"Adversity is an experience, not a final act."
- **Michael LeBoeuf, Ph.D.**

What 2-3 action items are you going to do today to be a more purposeful-leader?

1.

2.

3.

Tip #15: Connection is KEY!

Abraham Maslow studied it years and years ago with his *Hierarchy of Needs* Model. Everyone has basic human needs, but for one reason or another, it's easy to overlook these basic human needs with members of your team. Many times as leaders we are focused on what needs to get done, our "to-do" lists, and not so much on meeting the needs of team members.

Outside of basic physical needs, and our need for some level of security, probably the most important need we have is the need for connection. In other words, we need a sense of belongingness. All of us have varying levels of these needs; however, lack of fulfillment in any of these areas can result in a significant drop in employee engagement and productivity in your organization.

So, with that in mind, what are some of the things you do to connect with members of your team? What do you do for them that make them feel significant? What do you specifically that makes them understand they are a significant part of your team, and are a valuable asset to the organization?

The need for significance is important. Maslow defined it as our *Esteem* needs, and our need to *Self-Actualize*. The end result for employees who feel valued, significant, and connected to you and your organization is simple: improved productivity and loyalty.

Can you live with that?

Today's Leadership Intention

"Everybody ought to do at least two things each day that he or she hates to do, just for practice." **– William James**

What 2-3 action items are you going to do today to be a more purposeful-leader?

1.

2.

3.

Tip #16: Celebrate Your Victories!

In order to succeed in business and leadership long-term, it's essential that you have some "Wins" along the way. Unfortunately, it's easy to get caught up in the things that aren't going well, and miss out on the seemingly small things that may be driving your organization. You've heard it said over and over again that we shouldn't "sweat the small stuff." Well, when it comes to our successes, we should also live by this motto: "don't ignore the small stuff." Small victories are important. In fact, they can help drive momentum in your organization and for your team.

In the workplace, we tend to be very good about setting goals, creating action steps, and meeting deadlines; however, we are typically horrible about celebrating when we do achieve our goals. Find ways to celebrate with your team. When was the last team you exceeded a sales quota and celebrated by having lunch catered in, or by throwing a small party of some kind?

Your people, including yourself, have a strong desire to feel appreciated and valued. Appreciation and celebration go a long way when seeking to drive momentum in your organization and within your team for the long term.

Celebrate today!

Today's Leadership Intention

"Develop an attitude of gratitude and give thanks for everything that happens to you, knowing that every step forward is a step toward achieving something bigger and better than your current situation." **– Brian Tracy**

What 2-3 action items are you going to do today to be a more purposeful-leader?

1.

2.

3.

Tips #17: Be Fair to Your People

I have two small children. No pun intended, I hear my "fair share" of "That's not fair!" And I bet you do too! More often than not it comes with the territory in any position that requires a strong leadership role.

Although it's unrealistic to think we can create an environment where we will never hear this from some of our team members, there are things you can do as a leader to minimize an unfair workplace. For starters, the best leaders give their people frequent, constructive feedback. They also create opportunities for and support professional development within the organization. When I was in the corporate sector, we did performance evaluations once per year. Unfortunately, this amount of feedback was grossly insufficient for the demands and responsibilities we held in our positions.

I suggest that you offer feedback to members of your team at least monthly. Provide opportunities for members of your team to give you feedback as well. Upward feedback is not only empowering to your people, but it will give you invaluable feedback as to what's important to them, and how you can create a more fair, equitable environment.

Compensate fairly; promote fairly; be consistent in your leadership and management styles, and you will increase overall buy-in from members in your organization.

Today's Leadership Intention

"A great leader's courage to fulfill his vision comes from passion, not position." – **John Maxwell**

What 2-3 action items are you going to do today to be a more purposeful-leader?

1.

2.

3.

Tip #18: Leaders of Influence WIN!

John C. Maxwell says, "The true measure of leadership is influence - nothing more, nothing less." Many times when we think of leaders, we think of the high-profile executive with the office suite, cherry desk, and leather furniture. But in all reality, just because someone holds a high-level position in an organization does not necessarily make him or her a great leader.

Great leaders have influence. And great influencers have followers. I think it's time to put the idea out of our minds that leaders only exist in high-level positions. In this tough, dynamic business environment in which we live today, it's necessary that great leaders exist in all levels of the organization, not just at the top.

Leadership is not attained through a particular position or a particular pay grade. Leadership is influence, and leadership is earned. It's simply impossible to be a leader of any kind unless people are willing to step to the side and let you lead them because they believe in who you are, what you do, and what you seek to accomplish through them.

How can you influence someone in your organization today?

Today's Leadership Intention

"Only those who have learned the power of sincere and selfless contribution experience life's deepest joy: true fulfillment." – **Anthony Robbins**

What 2-3 action items are you going to do today to be a more purposeful-leader?

1.

2.

3.

Tip #19: Hire Partners, Not Employees

The company Zappos – they get it! They understand the importance of purpose. The purpose of the Zappos organization is "Delivering Happiness." In fact, their whole culture is founded upon this purpose.

One of the things I really admire about this company is this: when they hire help, they look for partners in a cause, not employees.

Zappos realizes that it's in their best interest to hire only those individuals who wholeheartedly buy-in to the purpose of the organization. Partners become long-term advocates for their brand; employees equate to short-term help.

The company believes in this so much that during their training process, if you don't believe you are a good fit for the organization they will pay you to leave. In fact, they will give you multiple chances to do so, and every time it's offered, the payment is a bit higher.

You see, Zappos realizes the hindrance of not having the right people on the bus. They understand the real costs associated with turnover. That's why the organization focuses on hiring long-term partners, not short-tem help!

Today's Leadership Intention

"Take action every day – some small dose at a time." **– Jeffrey Gitomer**

What 2-3 action items are you going to do today to be a more purposeful-leader?

1.

2.

3.

Tip #20: Foster a Culture of Innovation

Great leaders foster innovative cultures. In today's challenging, global marketplace, it's essential that team members in all levels of the organization are not only creative, but also innovative. And the good news is, it often boosts morale, workplace productivity and therefore, organizational profitability.

Successful leaders make innovation in the workplace a top priority. The challenge with innovation for many leaders is that it requires a willingness to take risks, manage adversity, and ultimately embrace the possibility for failure. Risk-averse cultures are not innovative! It's impossible for them to be. And for those organizations that embrace innovation, it's unrealistic for them to think that every innovative idea will prove successful or drive bottom-line results.

Innovation requires forward thinking. This is one of the main reasons why when I work with organizations in developing their business strategy, we look at a sixty-year window of time. We look at the last thirty years, and we look thirty years into the future. It's hard not to think innovatively when you look thirty years into the future and use that information to help your organization drive bottom-line results today.

So, to recap: 1) Make innovation a priority, 2) Take risks, and 3) Keep your eyes on the future.

Today's Leadership Intention

"Measure a person by the stretch of his imagination." – **Robert Schuller**

What 2-3 action items are you going to do today to be a more purposeful-leader?

1.

2.

3.

Tip #21: Knowing What to Measure

Just because I talk about the importance of purpose, does not mean that I don't understand the importance of profitability. I'm a businessman, and therefore I'm also a capitalist. And there are a lot of things that affect the overall profitability of your organization. One thing I've discovered in my career is this: great managers are not always great leaders; however, it's hard to find a great leader who also isn't a great manager. And you can't manage what you don't measure!

If you don't consistently measure those things that drive your organization, you don't know if they are getting better or worse. In all reality, you are trying to play the game of business in the dark. It simply doesn't work!

When I worked for a Fortune 50 company in the retail industry, we consistently measured activities that were extremely important in achieving the goals of the organization. We called them KPIs, or Key Performance Indicators, and as leaders and managers, we were held accountable for them.

Knowing what to measure is important. It's also important to communicate that information to members of your team. I think the majority of them want to know, and it's hard for them to be motivated to improve if they don't know how they are doing.

What are you measuring today?

Today's Leadership Intention

"The freedom to fail is vital if you're going to succeed." – **Michael Korda**

What 2-3 action items are you going to do today to be a more purposeful-leader?

1.

2.

3.

Tip #22: Be Decisive & Take Action

Faith without works is dead. Knowledge without implementation is useless. A commitment to leadership development without utilizing what has been learned is futile. Put one hundred leaders in a room at a training and development conference, and three of them will walk away and do something with it. These are the "three-percenters," the "high-achievers," the ones who literally transform organizations for the better.

Don't get me wrong, book knowledge and training is useful, but it doesn't make a great leader - only experience and taking action accomplish that! Great, effective leaders are willing to take what they have learned, and then transform it into ideas, visions, goals, and more importantly, decisions and actions. All the leadership development in the world is useless if the principles learned are not applied and followed-through on.

Effective leaders thoroughly examine what they've learned, and then think about how they can use that knowledge to improve their organization. Once the goals, strategies, and action steps have been established, they take consistent action until they are achieved. And that's one of the major reasons why they are great.

Action = Leadership Success...

Today's Leadership Intention

"Nothing good or great can be done in the absence of enthusiasm." **– Tom Peters**

What 2-3 action items are you going to do today to be a more purposeful-leader?

1.

2.

3.

Tip #23: Foster a Healthy Attitude

Each of us will confront difficulties in our life. These unwelcomed facets of life may range from the easily manageable to the overwhelmingly stressful. How well a person handles the stress imposed by these events is dependent on the attitude of the person. People who continue to feel "in control" despite what may feel like an "out-of-control" situation almost always recover faster. These people realize that there is value in the struggle.

So, what does a resilient attitude consist of? It is much more than saying, "Have a Nice Day!" For starters, it involves the willingness to be open to new ideas and situations – something the majority of us face often in our personal and professional lives.

People with a healthy attitude also tend to be very committed. This high level of commitment tends to result in people who are genuinely interested in life, and personal growth and development. In other words, they are engaged in life and work, and are therefore willing to grow and develop into new and exciting roles regardless of the challenges that may come with them.

Lastly, and perhaps the most important, is the sense of being in control. People with a high sense of control feel their decisions make a difference in the outcome of events, and even when confronted with challenges and stressors, they realize the can make a difference through their personal choices!

Today's Leadership Intention

"If you don't know where you're going, you will end up someplace else." **– Yogi Bera**

What 2-3 action items are you going to do today to be a more purposeful-leader?

1.

2.

3.

Tip #24: No "Animal Trainers" Allowed

Is traditional leadership as we know it working? A study released by the Gallup organization revealed that 62% of those in the workforce between the ages of 30 and 44 are disengaged. So, in answer to the question, I think not! When you think about it, traditional leadership and management involve motivating others in one of two ways: reward and punishment. In other words, *Animal Training*. The problem is reward and punishments are short-term answers to long-term problems. Realistically, we live in a world where raises and opportunity for advancement are not as prevalent as they were a decade ago. So, how do we keep team members engaged while minimizing turnover?

Some organizations today are experiencing major breakthroughs by focusing on leadership development programs that are designed to suit each individual's unique leadership style: What would happen if we changed today's leaders' perspective on what's really important? What would that look like? What would the results be in the organization if we got rid of the Animal Training philosophy and found a way to help people find purpose, meaning, and fulfillment in their work?

Personally, I think the results would be extraordinary. What do you think?

Today's Leadership Intention

"Success seems to be connected with action. Successful people keep moving. They make mistakes, but they don't quit." – **Conrad Hilton**

What 2-3 action items are you going to do today to be a more purposeful-leader?

1.

2.

3.

Tip #25: Develop a Heart for Serving

Successful leaders have a heart for serving others. And perhaps that's why they are so successful. Personally, I think it's a worthy concept for the majority of leaders today to reflect upon.

Are you trying to become the leader that others are really inspired to follow? If so, where is your heart when it comes to serving? I was in the corporate sector for more than a decade, and there were definitely times when I put my own interests ahead of the interests of those I was responsible of leading. I'm not saying I'm proud of that. All I'm saying is that there were times when I put the "Dangling Carrot" ahead of the interests of others. What about you?

John Maxwell in his book *The 21 Indispensable Qualities of a Leader* suggests that if we really desire to be the leader others want to follow, we must resolve this issue of servant-hood.

As Maxwell suggests, we should:
- Start listening to people
- Stop seeking advancement, and start taking risks for the benefit of others
- Stop seeking our own way, and start serving others

Perhaps we might even find purpose and fulfillment in the process!

Today's Leadership Intention

"No person was ever honored for what he received. Honor has been the reward for what he gave." – **Calvin Coolidge**

What 2-3 action items are you going to do today to be a more purposeful-leader?

1.

2.

3.

Tip #26: Is Your Door Always Open?

Have you ever worked for a supervisor who was always in the office and the door was always shut? I know I have! And notice I said Supervisor, not Leader.

The higher a person moves up in an organization, the more of a support-role they should play. Leaders are not meant to sit in the office and only invite team members in when there is an issue or concern. Instead, they should serve as a solid-foundation of support for the members of their team.

"Open Door Policies" not only create transparency in an organization, but they also give team members the opportunity to give constructive feedback to those who lead them. People need to know that their opinions and their concerns matter; and more importantly, that they will be follow-up on.

If you don't currently have an "Open Door Policy" in effect in your organization, you need to create this culture as quickly as possible.

Benefits of an "Open Door Policy" include:

- Improved communication between employees and members of management
- Empowered employees who feel they can seek the help of their direct supervisor
- The opportunity to receive upward feedback from those who report to you

Today's Leadership Intention

"When you know what you want and you want it badly enough, you will find the ways to get it." **– Jim Rohn**

What 2-3 action items are you going to do today to be a more purposeful-leader?

1.

2.

3.

Tip #27: The Power of "Thank You!"

"All I want is to feel appreciated. It doesn't have to be all the time, but at least once would be nice. No one here ever notices the hard work I put in day-in and day-out. My boss never ever says 'Thank You!' I guess what I do really isn't that important."

Have you ever felt this way? If you're human, I guarantee you that you have. And if you disagree with me, I'd quickly call you a liar. Every single human being desires to feel appreciated; valued; that what they do is significant and important. And the easiest way to meet that need is by simply saying "Thank You," and meaning it!

The words *Thank* and *You* when used together are probably the most powerful words you would ever desire to hear from a leader in the workplace. The only other phrase that is more powerful is "I Love You," and in many cases in the workplace, that's inappropriate, but you get my drift.

Leading others isn't rocket science; although at times we make it that way. Everyone welcomes the words "Thank You." When we don't hear these words at all, it's easy for us to feel that we are being taken for granted. When we hear them all of the time, they lack sincerity, meaning and significance.

Find ways to incorporate a "Thank You" to someone on your team every single day. As a leader, it gives you the opportunity to look for things that are being done well and right too, not things to criticize.

Today's Leadership Intention

"Every great business is built on friendship."
– JC Penny

What 2-3 action items are you going to do today to be a more purposeful-leader?

1.

2.

3.

Tip #28: Take Responsibility for your Outcomes

I'm amazed at how some people can get an amazing amount of stuff done in a very short time. I'm also amazed at the number of people I've met through the years who say they are going to do this or that, but for one reason or another never get started. Do you find yourself at times procrastinating? Avoiding a difficult conversation that should have happened weeks ago? If so, you aren't doing anyone any favors.

Momentum is important, and it has a dramatic effect business results and our ability to lead others. One of the biggest stumbling blocks to creating and sustaining momentum is the unwillingness to take action and to take responsibility. Like it or not, help isn't coming anytime soon. Yes, the things on your "To-Do List" resting squarely on your shoulders.

I'm not trying to be negative in any way. And I'm not saying that I don't believe in the value of teamwork. All I'm saying is as a leader, when you hold yourself accountable for your outcomes, it can be very liberating; even if you're working with other members in your organization.

Taking responsibility and consistent action doesn't mean you shouldn't involve others to achieve success in your organization. However, it does show that you care, and that you have an obligation to take action and to deliver results.

Today's Leadership Intention

"The best time to plant a tree is 20 years ago. The second best time is now." **- Chinese Proverb**

What 2-3 action items are you going to do today to be a more purposeful-leader?

1.

2.

3.

Tip# 29: Develop Core Competencies

I've taught many business management and marketing courses at the college level. And in those courses, we talk a lot about things like strengths, weaknesses, opportunities, and threats. We also talk about core competencies. When I think of core competencies, I think of those specific things that make your organization unique; those things that separate it from the competition; those things that create a sustainable competitive advantage in your industry.

We usually look at core competencies from an organizational perspective, but members of your team have their own core competencies as well. Those specific things about them that make them unique; those things that separate them from others team members in your organization; those things that make them invaluable in the workplace.

One thing I noticed during my tenure in the corporate sector is that organizations all too often focus on the weaknesses or opportunities for improvement with their team members, not on the core competencies.

What would happen to your organization if you identified the core competencies of each member of your team and you leveraged those in an effort to maximize talent, efficiency and productivity in the workplace? I bet your employees would be happier, more loyal, more innovative, and more productive!

Today's Leadership Intention

"Success is achieved by developing our strengths, not by eliminating our weaknesses." - **Marilyn Vos Savant**

What 2-3 action items are you going to do today to be a more purposeful-leader?

1.

2.

3.

Tip #30: Become a Mentor or Coach

Look back over your life and your career. Who has been there at various points along the way that has served as a great mentor or coach for you? Wonderful things can happen in your career and your life when you find the right mentor. A lot of wonderful things can happen for others in your organization too when you, as their leader, show a willingness to serve as a mentor or coach to those with significant potential.

Many successful business owners, and many successful leaders throughout history, have had the opportunity to be mentored by other extraordinary business owners and leaders.

One of the great values I've learned by having the opportunity to learn from my mentors, is that I've learned lessons I may never have had the opportunity to learn otherwise. I've had the opportunity to learn from their successes, and more importantly, I've had the opportunity to learn from their mistakes and their failures; invaluable knowledge, considering I was unlikely to make the same ones they made!

My success as an entrepreneur and business owner completely changed when a more tenured consultant named Jim Whitt made the decision to take me "under their wing," serve as a mentor, and give back for the success they've had. And for that, I'm eternally grateful.

Who will you become a mentor to today?

Today's Leadership Intention

"Tell me and I forget, teach me and I may remember, involve me and I learn."
- Benjamin Franklin

What 2-3 action items are you going to do today to be a more purposeful-leader?

1.

2.

3.

About the Author

Nathan R Mitchell is America's Leading Empowerment Coach, and the founder of Clutch Consulting. He is an experienced business and leadership development coach, author, and speaker. Nathan helps career professionals, executives, and business owners become better leaders and become more engaged in the workplace by finding purpose, meaning, and fulfillment in the work they do.

He holds a Bachelor of Science Degree in Entrepreneurship, an MBA from Missouri State University, and Certifications in Professional Coaching, Behaviors, and Motivators Analysis. After graduating from college, he took an operations management position with a Fortune 50 company where he had eleven years of success before leaving to pursue other endeavors.

In 2010 he started Clutch Consulting with one simple purpose: "Growing Businesses and Empowering People." Nathan loves affecting change, mentoring others, creating new ideas and innovative ways of doing things, giving others perspective, and helping companies have better bottom lines.

If you are interested in consulting, training programs, workshops, or speaking engagements for your organization, simply contact Nathan R Mitchell:

>Phone: 918.851.7246
>Online: NathanRMitchell.com
>ClutchConsulting.net

Sign up for Nathan's FREE, Weekly E-Newsletter at NathanRMitchell.com

Book Order Form

If you would like to order Nathan Mitchell's book *Leading with Purpose: 30 Empowering Tips to Transform Your Organization* for members of your team or organization, fill out the form below and mail to:

Nathan R Mitchell
PO Box 2818
Broken Arrow, OK 74013
918.851.7246

Name: _____

Address: _____

City: _____

State: _____

Zip Code: _____

Phone: _____

Email: _____

Continued on Next Page...

Type of Card: _____

Credit Card Number: _____

Expiration Date: _____

3-Digit Security Code: _____

Quantity of Books You Would Like: _____

Total Price: ($14.95 x Qty. Ordered) _____

TOTAL PRICE INCLUDES S&H
THANK YOU FOR YOUR ORDER!!!

Company Checks Are Also Accepted...

Please allow 3-4 weeks for delivery. Should it take longer, we will contact you as soon as possible.

Made in the USA
Charleston, SC
06 January 2017